Willia
th
CONQU

the epic adventure

Today, you are visiting an extremely old site or monument dating back to the period when a very important person reigned over Normandy: William the Conqueror.
But do you know who William was?
Let's read the following text before going on to enjoy the activities. It will help you to get to know him a bit better.

William's father, Robert « the Magnificent », was Duke Richard's brother and lived in Falaise Castle. One day, next to a fountain, he noticed a very pretty young girl called Arlette. He fell immediately in love with her and they married and had two children: William and Adelaide.
So, William was born in Falaise Castle in 1027, nearly a thousand years ago. The castle has changed a lot since then. Many constructions have been added, in particular an impressive keep*.
Upon Richard's death, Robert became Duke of Normandy. Then, in 1035, it was William's turn. However, he was but a young boy and had to face conspiracies and attacks by powerful lords who were looking to take his place.
At the age of twenty, William fought against and was victorious over these lords at a place called Val-ès-Dunes, near Caen. Hence, he enforced his rights upon the dukedom his father had left him. The young duke could now freely govern over what he hoped would be a peaceful, rich and powerful dukedom.

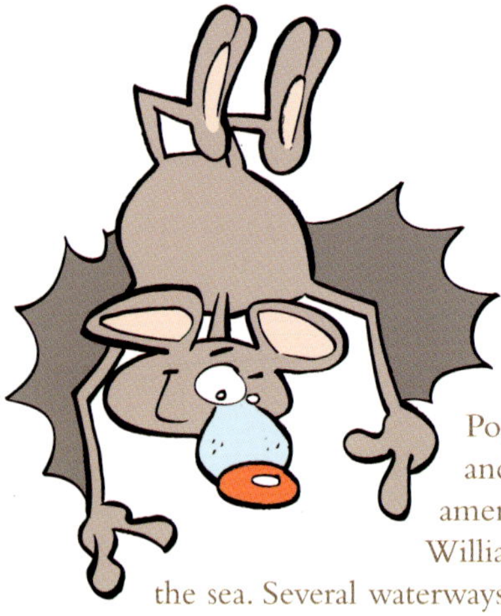

Towards 1050, William married Matilda, the daughter of Baldwin V, Count of Flanders and King Henry I of France's niece. The Pope was hostile to their marriage since William and Matilda were distant cousins. To make amends, he asked each of them to build an abbey*. William chose the town of Caen, a few miles from the sea. Several waterways flow through the town, including the River Orne and there is also a port, together with fine limestone deposits. Positioned in the heart of William's dukedom, Caen was, indeed, the ideal strategic location for building an impressive castle to house the ducal powers. Hence, William made Caen his second capital and he encouraged the town's development. **The ducal castle has been enlarged over the centuries. It is one of Europe's largest walled castles and today it still houses the vestiges of William's palace. The two Benedictine abbeys* founded by William (the Men's Abbey) and Matilda (the Ladies' Abbey) are today home to the town and the regional councils.**

William was by then one of Europe's most influential figures. He developed his dukedom, regularly defending it against his adversaries. He also wanted to conquer other lands...
Across the Channel, the very old King Edward the Confessor was close to death. Since he had no children, he had to choose between his brother-in-law Harold and his cousin William of Normandy to succeed him to the throne. He chose William and sent Harold to Normandy to inform him...
In Bayeux, William asked Harold to swear loyalty to him over holy relics: Harold had no choice but to let William reign over England. However, upon Edward's death, Harold forgot his oath and accepted to be crowned King of England. William was furious and wanted to regain his inheritance. He gathered together thousands of soldiers, had hundreds of boats built and landed in England late September in the year

1066. On the 14th of October, to the north of the small port of Hastings, William's troops confronted Harold's. The battle lasted one day. Harold was killed and William was victorious.

The Bayeux Tapestry recounts this story. This remarkable work dates back to William's period. It is a 70 metre long by 50 centimetre high embroidery which Odo, Bishop of Bayeux and William's half-brother, is said to have had embroidered to adorn the nave of Bayeux Cathedral.

William was crowned King of England on the 25th of December 1066. He who had been referred to as "the Bastard", had become "the Conqueror". Founder of a highly powerful Anglo-Norman kingdom envied by many, William died in Rouen on the 9th of September 1087, four years after the death of Matilda. Both are buried in Caen: Matilda in the Ladies' Abbey and William in the Men's Abbey.

Their descendents reigned over Normandy and England, including **Henry I Beauclerc** who had the keep* and the Hall of the Exchequer* built in Caen Castle, together with the great square keep* in Falaise Castle; **Henry II Plantagenet** who, upon his marriage with Eleanor, added the region of Aquitaine to his Anglo-Norman kingdom; **Richard the Lionheart**, then his brother **John Lackland** who, in 1204, was to lose Normandy which was then attached to the French crown. This date was to mark the end of the fabulous epic of the Dukes of Normandy...

Your guides

The fox,
whose name is **WILY**,
is the most learned of the band.

He appears at the beginning of each chapter to introduce places, their history, their particularities and their link with the story of William the Conqueror.

For certain questions, he can also provide you with further information in the form of balloons or boxes.

The crow is called **WAZZAT**, and asks you questions throughout the booklet.

The bat, nicknamed **SHERLOCK**, gives you the answers in the central notebook. He also provides you with useful hints throughout the activities.

Activity booklet How to use it

On the inside cover

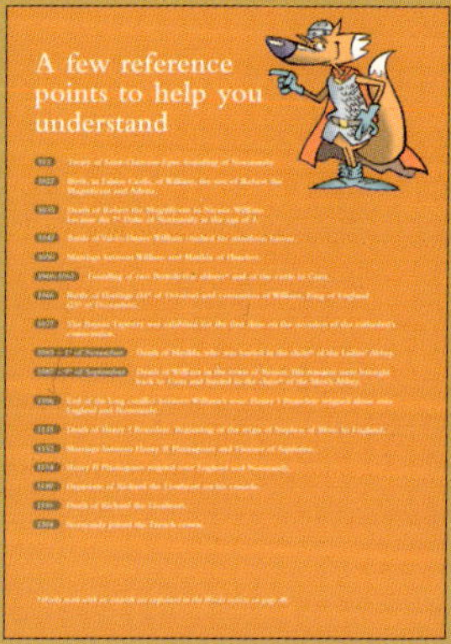

The dates help you to find your bearings.

For each site

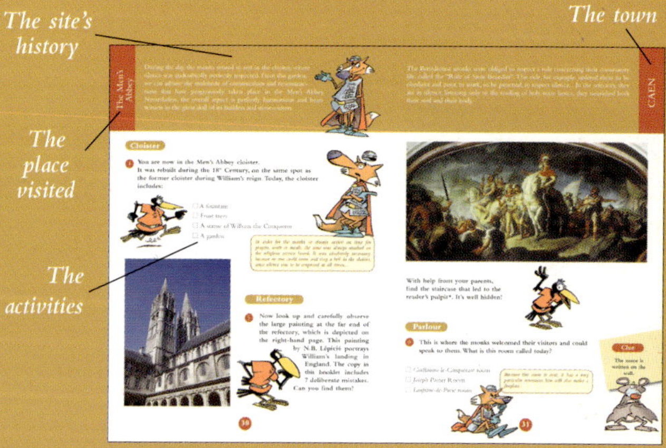

3 double pages.

In the central notebook

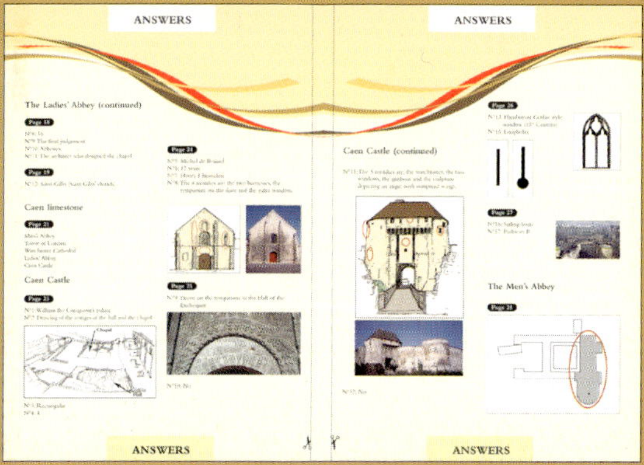

Answers.

At the end of the booklet

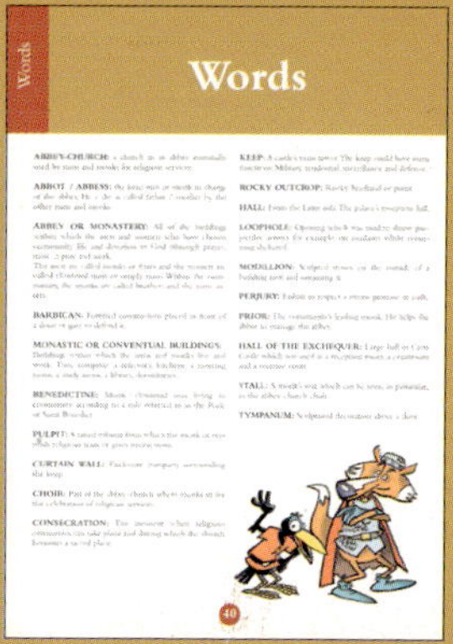

Difficult words are marked with an asterisk and explained on page 40.

The 3 TOWNS to discover

Bayeux

The Bayeux Tapestry Museum offers visitors the possibility to discover the famous 11th Century embroidery recounting, over 70 metres, the story of the Norman Conquest.
The tapestry can be considered as one of history's very first comic strips.

The town's cathedral housed the Tapestry for many years. Odo (William the Conqueror's half-brother) was Bishop of Bayeux and was behind the Tapestry's creation.

Caen

William had the castle and two abbeys* built there. Thus, he established his power.
He is buried in the Men's Abbey.
His wife, Matilda, is buried in the Ladies' Abbey.

Falaise

William's birthplace. The castle combined both military and residential functions. Its two square keeps* are among the rare remaining examples of Anglo-Norman architecture on the Continent.

The Bayeux Tapestry Museum

History's very first comic strip, the Bayeux Tapestry tells the story of the conquest of England by William, Duke of Normandy in 1066. This story was embroidered during the Middle Ages with woollen yarn on an immense canvas measuring around 70 metres in length. William's half-brother, Odo, was Bishop of Bayeux. A short while after the conquest, he ordered the tapestry to be embroidered by English monks for it to be displayed in Bayeux Cathedral. This medieval masterpiece is unique throughout the world and you can come and admire it at the Bayeux Tapestry Museum: here's the story it tells...

On the ground floor, you will discover the masterpiece which is listed in UNESCO's Memory of the World International Register. Look at the different scenes and answer the following questions:

1 Which event does the Bayeux Tapestry recount?

- ☐ The conquest of England by King Harold
- ☐ The conquest of Normandy by William the Conqueror
- ☐ The conquest of England by William the Conqueror

2 Which of these details can you see on the scene?

☐ 1

☐ 2

☐ 3

3 How does the Bayeux Tapestry end?

- ☐ A great feast and a ball are organised in Bayeux
- ☐ King Harold is killed
- ☐ Duke William is crowned King of England

In 1064, Edward, the very old King of England had no children and, since they were cousins, chose William, Duke of Normandy to succeed him to the throne. Edward asked Harold, a powerful English lord, to go and inform William. Harold swore that he would be faithful to William; however, despite his oath, he took the throne upon the death of Edward. William could not accept such perjury*. Descended from the Vikings, he ordered the construction of a huge fleet of ships to cross the English Channel armed with soldiers and horses. The ships' prows, decorated with dragonheads, arrived on the English shores in September 1066 and, a few days later, on the 14th of October, the Norman troops defeated Harold's army at the Battle of Hastings. William was no longer only Duke of Normandy, but had also become King of England...

4 **Among the following tools, which one does not appear on this scene from the Bayeux Tapestry?**

After the Battle of Hastings, England was transformed: the Saxon lords who owned castles and land were replaced by William's companions, the Norman lords. The new king brought a new architectural style to England and had castles and cathedrals built using white Caen limestone; the Tower of London is a fine example!

In the first floor exhibition room, you can discover several scale models. Look carefully and answer the following questions.

5

What goods is this boat transporting?

- ☐ Stone
- ☐ Sugar
- ☐ Containers

6 **Carefully look at the feudal *motte* (mound). Which material was used to built these early fortified castles dating from the 10th and 11th Centuries?**

- ☐ Stone
- ☐ Wood
- ☐ Bricks

7

What church is this?

- ☐ Bayeux Cathedral
- ☐ Winchester Cathedral
- ☐ Saint-Stephen's abbey-church in Caen

As for the Tapestry, it was to remain within Bayeux Cathedral up to the French Revolution in 1789, protected within a wooden chest when it was not unrolled to be displayed to the local inhabitants.

8 **Maps and a few drawings offer you geographical and historical clues. Find the names of the towns on the maps.**

In England

1 B ....

2 C ....

3 D ....

4 H ....

5 L ....

6 P ....

7 Y ....

In France

8 B ....

9 C ....

10 D ....

11 D ....

12 F ....

13 The M........................

14 R ....

15 St V ....

The Cathedral

In the Christian faith, the bishop is in charge of a territory referred to as the diocese and his church is called a cathedral. The cathedral in Bayeux was built between 1030 and 1077 and was completed by William's half-brother, Odo of Conteville, Bishop of Bayeux. It was very probably Odo who ordered for the Bayeux Tapestry to be embroidered in order to explain to all of the local inhabitants why and how William had conquered England. On the 14th of July 1077, William and Matilda were present alongside Odo to celebrate the cathedral's consecration*.

9 The bishop of Bayeux, Odo of Conteville (1049-1097), half-brother to William the Conqueror, Duke of Normandy supervised the construction of his cathedral. That's where his throne can be found: the cathedra. What name is given to a bishop's church?

☐ Abbey-church ☐ Basilica ☐ Cathedral

10 In what way were William and Odo related?

☐ Odo was William's half-brother
☐ Odo was William's cousin
☐ Odo was William's uncle

11 Before entering the church, take a close look at the monument. On which exterior part of the building can you still see Roman arches?

☐ The portals

☐ The central tower

☐ The facade towers

The Tapestry was displayed in the cathedral nave a few days each year, then was folded and kept in a chest. It was extremely lucky since, in 1105 and 1160, two fires almost totally destroyed the cathedral. For the same reason, the two towers situated at the main entrance are the only remaining elements of Odo's original cathedral. When, in 1476, a list was compiled of the cathedral's contents, the Tapestry was mentioned, providing the oldest proof of its presence in Bayeux.

12 **When you enter into the cathedral nave, you will discover a sculpted scene from the Bayeux Tapestry. What does this scene depict?**

☐ Edward sending Harold to Normandy

☐ Harold's oath

☐ Harold's coronation

13 **The Tapestry was intended to be exhibited inside the cathedral a few days each year. Where was it kept the rest of the year?**

☐ In a wooden chest

☐ In a cupboard

☐ In the crypt

Clue

Read Wily's explanation at the top of the page and you'll find out where the Tapestry was kept.

Built on the summit of a hill, the Ladies' Abbey housed Benedictine★ nuns from its very beginning. In charge of the nuns, there was an abbess★ who was often from one of Normandy's noblest families. The very first abbess★ was called Mathilde des Préaux and was the Duke of Normandy, William the Bastard's great aunt. The second, Cecily, was one of the ducal couple's daughters. She was offered to the Abbey★ on the day of the consecration mass celebrated

The visit starts in the visitors' reception hall where the guide will explain the history of the Ladies' Abbey to you in a few minutes. Listen carefully because he or she will, in only a few minutes, give you a summary of over 9 centuries of history. You will then go through to the cloister and visit a few different rooms (washbasins, kitchens...) before entering the Holy Trinity abbey-church★. You will see the church's founder, Matilda's grave in the church choir★.

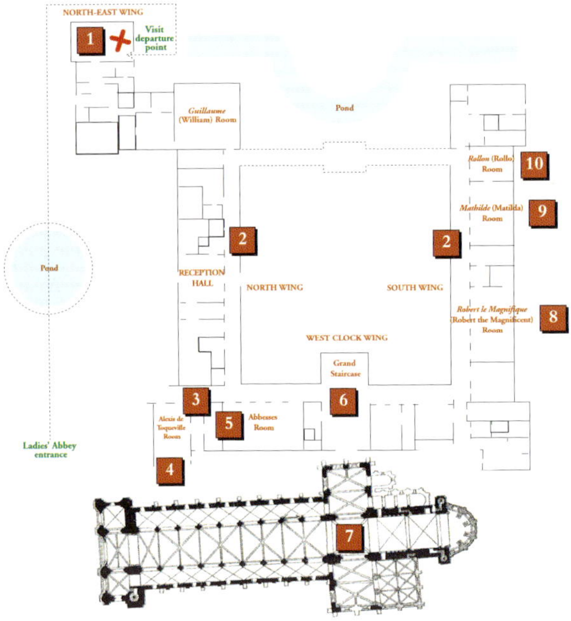

Map of the visit

1 Visitors' reception hall
2 Cloister
3 Lavatorium
4 Kitchens
5 Refectory
6 Great vestibule
7 Holy Trinity abbey-church
8 Chapter house
9 Library
10 Study room

You can then try to imagine, thanks to your guide's explanations, what the building looked like at the time of Matilda, before learning of the many transformations which have been made over the following centuries. You will also be allowed to visit the crypt. When you come back up into the church, don't forget to lower your head, people were much smaller in the Middle Ages. Back inside the 18th Century convent, you will visit a few rooms in the south wing of the cloister, such as the chapter house or the library.

on the 18th of June 1066, when she was around 5 years old. She became abbess* as from 1113. During her abbotship, she bore the title of Madame de Caen, a title which was to be given to all of her succeeding abbesses*. She died in 1127 and was buried next to her mother. A few of her bones are today preserved in the abbey crypt.
The ducal couple gave birth to ten children, four of whom were boys (Robert Curthose, Richard, William Rufus and Henry Beauclerc) and six girls (Agatha, Cecily, Adela, Constance, Adelicia and Matilda).

1 **Who was the abbey-church's founder?**

- ☐ Adele of Blois
- ☐ Matilda of Flanders
- ☐ Cecily of France

2 **Why did William and Matilda found the Caen abbeys?**

- ☐ They were very rich
- ☐ To obtain the pope's pardon
- ☐ To be buried there

Clue

Carefully look at the painting of the Abbess* Anne de Montmorency, because she recovered this object. This painting hangs in the great vestibule.

3 **Which precious object disappeared from the Queen's grave during its desecration in 1562?**

Answer : ....

The abbey's★ founder died on the 1st of November 1083. According to her last wishes, she was buried in the abbey-church★ choir. A shrine, surmounted by a black Tournai marble stone, was created to receive her remains. Certain authors refer to a recumbent statue of the queen which is said to have been placed on the stone; however no illustration has ever been found.
The inscription engraved in the marble stone reminds us of the queen's noble origin and of her qualities. The last sentence tells how she endeavoured to help the poor and, for that reason, she deserved eternal life.

4 **Mark with a dot or a cross the location of the founder's grave. Using the map to help you, find the Gothic chapel.**

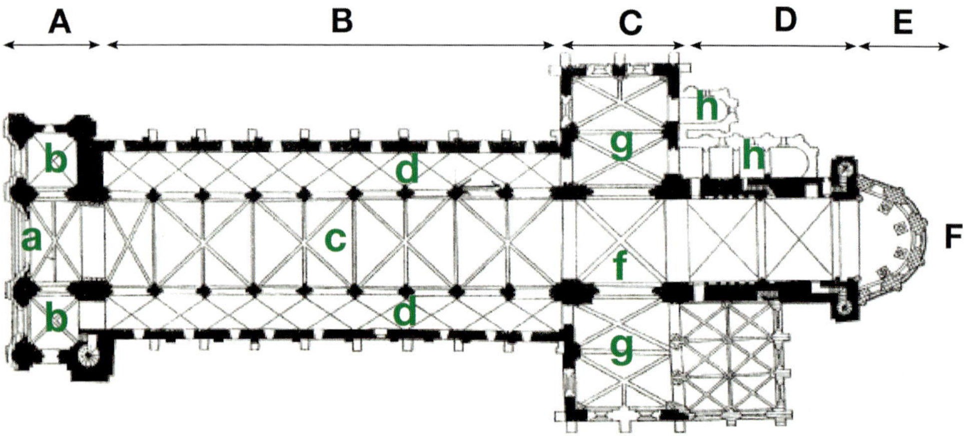

- a Porch
- b Tower
- c Central body (or vessel) of the nave
- d Collateral nave or aisle
- f Transept crossing
- g Transept arm
- h Apsidiole

- A Narthex
- B 3 vessel nave
- C Transept
- D Choir★
- E Apse
- F Chevet

In 1100, on his return from a crusade, her son Robert Curthose came to meditate her grave and left standards there which he had taken from the Saracens. The grave was desecrated during the Wars of Religion (in May 1562), but the queen's bones remained intact.
A few fragments were exhumed in 1959 to be studied. The study revealed that she was small in size, measuring no more than 1.5 metres (4 feet 9 inches). In 1965, they were returned to the church choir* under their original stone.

Looking at the gravestone, find the names of the founder and of William in the inscription.

Clue

In French, Matilda is written "Mathilde".

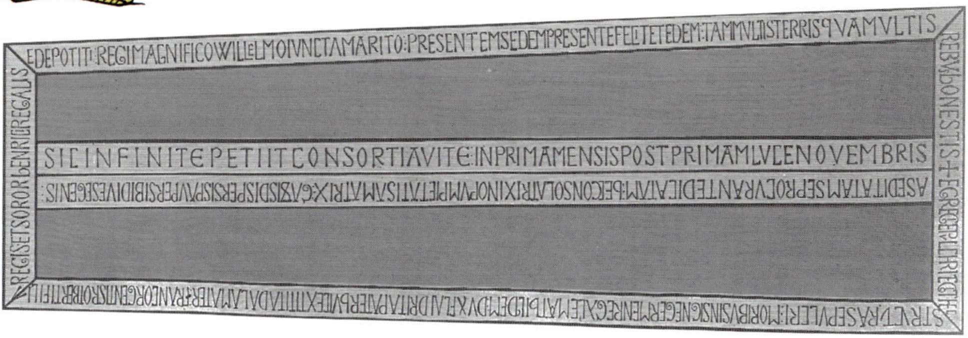

6 **Which animal did the sculpture try to depict?**

Answer: ....

7 **What source of inspiration did the sculptor of the apse capitals use?**
(2 possible answers)

- ☐ The crusades
- ☐ A book referred to as a bestiary
- ☐ Internet
- ☐ Magazines

The original Holy Trinity abbey-church, built between 1060 and 1080 was smaller and was in keeping with a traditional Benedictine plan. A porch open on either side was used as an entrance (on the south facade tower, there are still traces of an arch). The choir* was shorter ending just behind the queen's grave. As for the elevation, the first church only had one level of high arches in the nave, covered with a visible wooden framework. The building, just like most Romanesque churches, was very dark. Norman

8 How many columns can you find in the crypt:

Answer: ....

9 What story does the capital at the current entrance to the crypt tell?

☐ The legend of Icarus
☐ The final judgement
☐ The origin of Batman

10 Who's bones are preserved in the crypt?

☐ Norman dukes
☐ Abbesses
☐ Bishops

11 Which man is represented in the Gothic chapel?

☐ The owner of the abbey
☐ The architect who designed the chapel
☐ One of the abbey guides

Clue

Look up and you'll see him climbing up one of the arches.

architects nevertheless developed the concept of "lantern towers". Built at the transept crossing, the lantern tower had large openings allowing daylight to enter into the church, hence facilitating the holy readings.
On each transept arm, apsidioles were built to be used as chapels. The first changes were made as early as the late 11th Century with, in particular, the construction of a crypt upon which an apse was built, then the ribbed nave vaulting between 1120 and 1130. It is under these very vaults that the nuns' voices have resounded in song for several centuries.

12 **The ruins of a church are located next to the Holy Trinity. Which church is it?**

- ☐ *Saint-Etienne-le-Vieux* (Old St Stephen's church)
- ☐ *Saint-Pierre* (Saint Peter's church)
- ☐ *Saint-Gilles* (Saint Giles' church)

PORTRAITS OF WILLIAM

Very few documents dating from the 11th Century offer precise portraits of William the Conqueror. The Bayeux Tapestry, an indispensable masterpiece recounting the story of the Norman Conquest, provides us with valuable information on the period's dress and hairstyles.

These documents offer complementary details on what a typical medieval character may have looked like, but there is nothing really specific in the realism with which the portraits were represented. William was described as being taller than average. In any case, William has provided, throughout the centuries, a source of inspiration to many artists and a number of portraits of him can be found.
One thing is certain; he must have been extremely strong-minded and determined to succeed as he did in the many projects he undertook.

Bayeux Tapestry
William and Harold's oath.

Fresco, disappeared from
Saint Stephen's church and drawn
by Ducarel,
Antiquités anglo-normandes, 1827.

Falaise.
Statue by Rochet.

Saint Stephen's Church in Caen.
Portrait by
Saint-Martin-de-Fontenay.

Bayeux Tapestry
Mannequin displayed
on the first floor
(exhibition hall).

Sculpture above the entrance
to a building located
in Place Reine Mathilde,
opposite the Ladies' Abbey.

The Bayeux Tapestry Museum

Page 8

N°1: The conquest of England by William the Conqueror
N°2: 1
N°3: King Harold is killed

Page 9

N°4: 2

Page 10

N°5: Stone
N°6: Wood
N°7: Winchester Cathedral

Page 11

N°8:

In England	In France
1 Bosham	8 Bayeux
2 Canterbury	9 Caen
3 Dover	10 Dives-sur-Mer
4 Hastings	11 Dol
5 London	12 Falaise
6 Pevensey	13 The Mont-St-Michel
7 York	14 Rouen
	15 St Valéry-sur-Somme

Page 12

N°9: The cathedral
N°10: Odo was William's half-brother
N°11: The facade towers

Page 13

N°12: Harold's oath
N°13: In a wooden chest

The Ladies' Abbey

Page 15

N°1: Matilda of Flanders
N°2: To obtain the pope's pardon
N°3: A gold ring set with a sapphire

Page 16

N°4: The location of the founder's grave and the Gothic chapel.

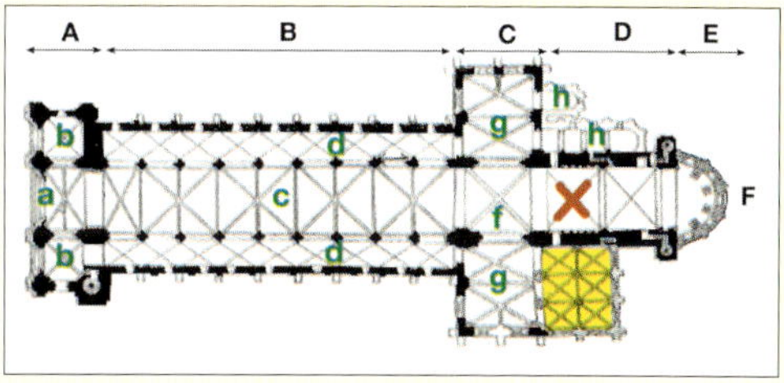

Page 17

N°5: Inscription bearing the name of the founder (Mathilde) and of William (Willelm)

N°6: An elephant
N°7: The crusades, a book referred to as a bestiary

The Ladies' Abbey (continued)

Page 18

N°8: 16
N°9: The final judgement
N°10: Abbesses
N°11: The architect who designed the chapel

Page 19

N°12: *Saint-Gilles* (Saint Giles' church)

Caen limestone

Page 21

Men's Abbey
Tower of London
Winchester Cathedral
Ladies' Abbey
Caen Castle

Caen Castle

Page 23

N°1: William the Conqueror's palace
N°2: Drawing of the vestiges of the hall and the chapel

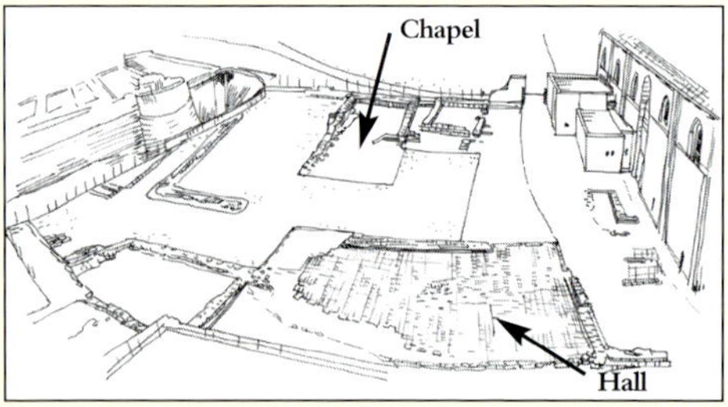

N°3: Rectangular
N°4: 4

Page 24

N°5: Michel de Boüard
N°6: 17 years
N°7: Henry I Beauclerc
N°8: The 4 mistakes are: the two buttresses, the tympanum on the door and the extra window.

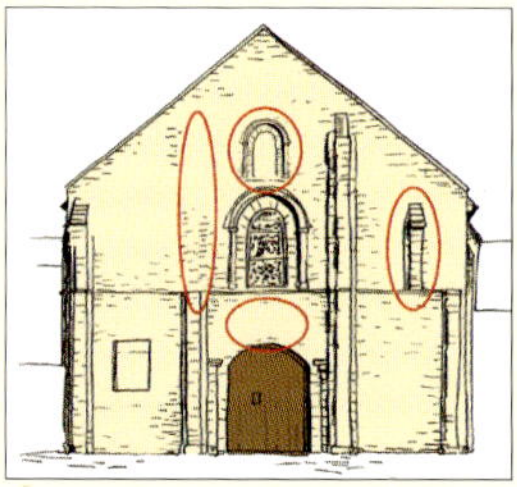

Page 25

N°9: Decor on the tympanum in the Hall of the Exchequer:

N°10: No

Caen Castle (continued)

N°11: The 5 mistakes are: the watchtower, the two windows, the gunboat and the sculpture depicting an angel with outspread wings.

N°12: No

Page 26

N°13: Flamboyant Gothic style window (15th Century)

N°15: Loopholes:

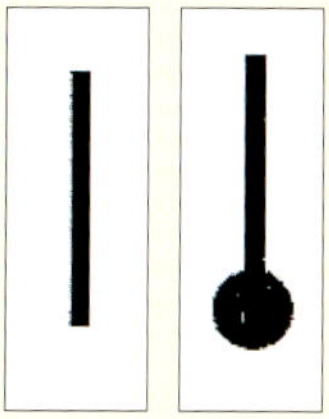

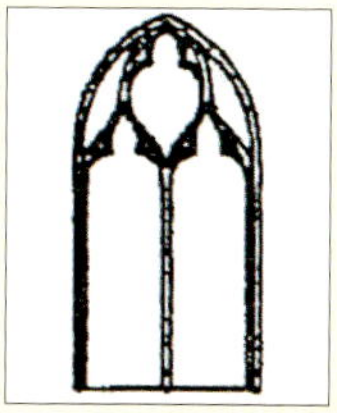

Page 27

N°16: Sailing boats

N°17: Barbican B

The Men's Abbey

Page 28

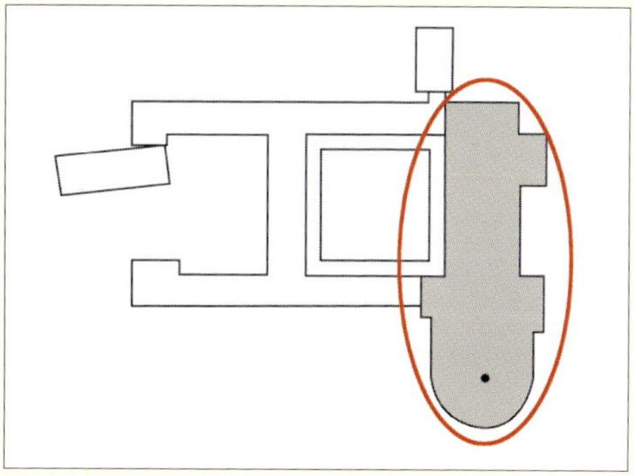

ANSWERS

Page 29

N°1: A dove
N°2: Jesus and Mary
N°3: B

Page 31

N°6: *Joseph Poirier* Room

Page 32

N°7: Missing elements from the abbey-church facade:

Page 33

N°8: 3 levels
(the high arches surmounted by galleries, then, on the very top, the high windows).
N°9: 1087 written MLXXXVII
This was the year of William's death.

Page 30

N°4 : A (French style) garden

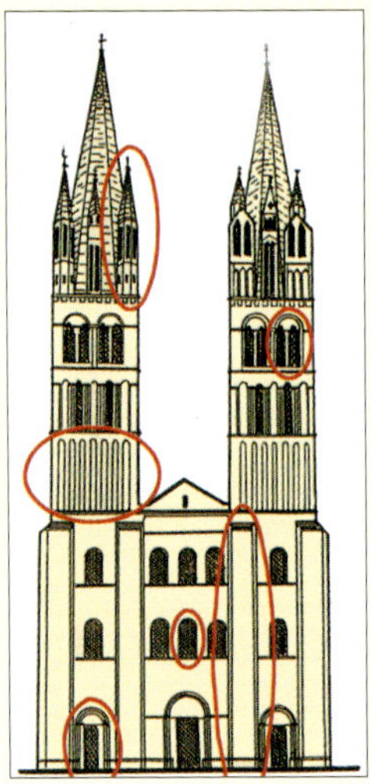

Falaise Castle

Page 35

N°1: Metal and concrete
N°2: No

Page 36

N°3: Latrines (toilets)

Page 37

N°4: Henry Plantagenet and Eleanor of Aquitaine
N°5: Christmas

Page 38

N°6: Answer to the riddle:
F = Ph + il + IP (VIP without the "V") = Philip
N°7: The camera was the place reserved for the lord and his family's private living quarters
N°8: Latin

Page 39

N°8: *Rollon* (Rollo) (911-933)
Guillaume Longue-Épée (William Longsword) (933-942)
Richard sans Peur (Richard the Fearless) (942-966)
Richard le Bon (Richard the Good) (996-1026)
Richard Trois (Richard III) (1026-1027)
Robert le Magnifique (Robert the Magnificent) (1027-1035)
Guillaume le Conquérant (William the Conqueror) (1035-1087)

CAEN LIMESTONE

Caen limestone was used to build many edifices during William the Conqueror's reign. This stone is actually not only extracted in Caen, but also in the surrounding countryside. It was formed from a limestone bed which is over 150 million years old. This bed stretches from Bayeux to Falaise and is 20 kilometres (12 miles) wide.

It is renowned throughout many regions across the globe and is still used to build many monuments.
The limestone quarries in and around the town of Caen alone cover over 400 hectares!
So, as you can see, our ancestors genuinely "delved" deep down to offer us the beautiful buildings you can admire today.

If you have carefully paid attention to each visit, you should be able to name the following buildings made of Caen limestone.

M ________ A ________

T______ of L ________

W________ C ________

L ________ A ________

C ________ C ________

The Ducal Castle

Caen Castle was built around 1060 by William the Conqueror on a rocky outcrop* dominating a marshy valley where the River Orne and its tributaries flow. At the time, this vast castle housed the ducal palace and the parish of Saint George together with its church. At the foot of the imposing castle, the town of Caen gradually developed. The construction of the Men's Abbey and the Ladies' Abbey on either side of the castle transformed Caen into one of the most important towns in the dukedom.

The activities in this booklet are designed to be carried out on your own, but under the watchful eye of your parents. They will lead you to discover Caen Castle which was built by William the Conqueror.
The following castle map will help to find your way around. So, remember to study it carefully!

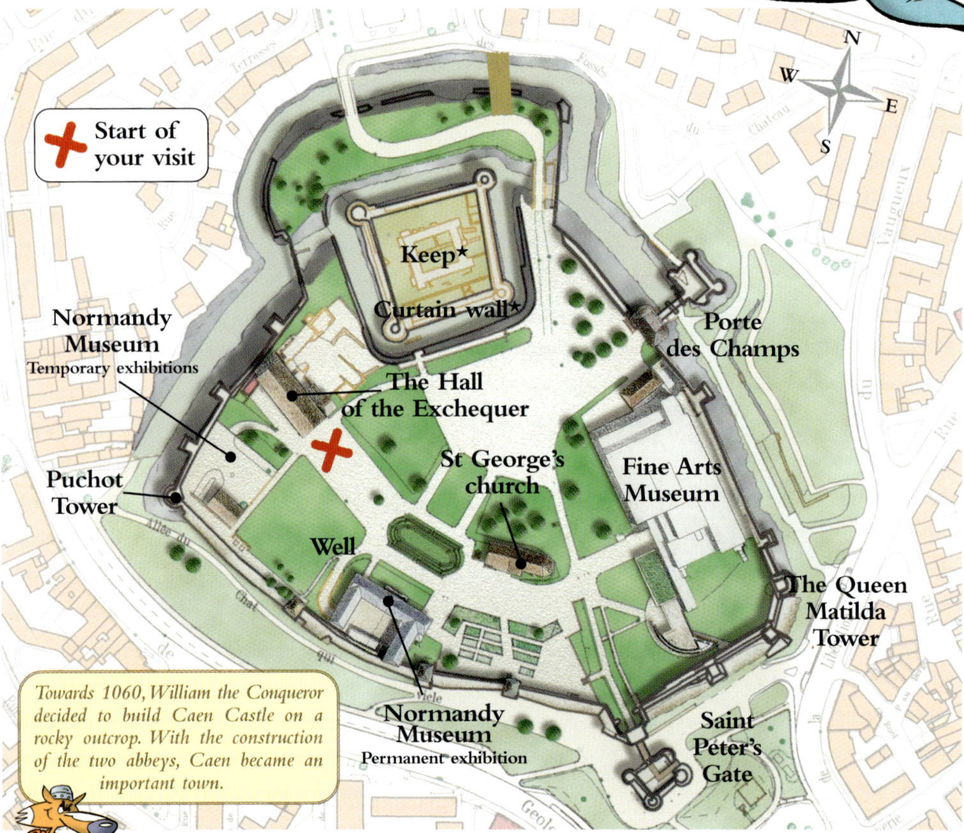

Towards 1120, Henry I Beauclerc, William the Conqueror's son, had a keep* built to the north next to the main castle gate. This daunting square tower measured over 25 metres in height, but has today, unfortunately, disappeared. The Hall of the Exchequer* was built during the same period; a splendid reception hall of Romanesque architecture completing William the Conqueror's palace, but in a more modest dimension.

1 Find the display panel next to the railings. Read it carefully and find which buildings used to stand here:

- ☐ A fire station
- ☐ William the Conqueror's palace
- ☐ The former Normandy Museum

2 Go past the railings and up onto the rampart. Stop at the first level. Look at the photograph of the ducal palace on the display panel and add the vestiges of the hall* and the chapel to the drawing.

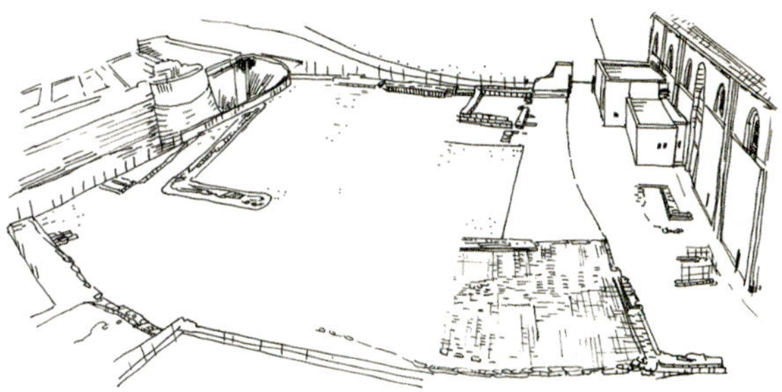

3 Now go up onto the belvedere on the top of the ramparts. Look at the keep* surrounded by its curtain wall*. What shape do you think the keep* was:

- ☐ Round
- ☐ Rectangular
- ☐ Octagonal

4 How many towers are there in the curtain wall*?

Answer: ....

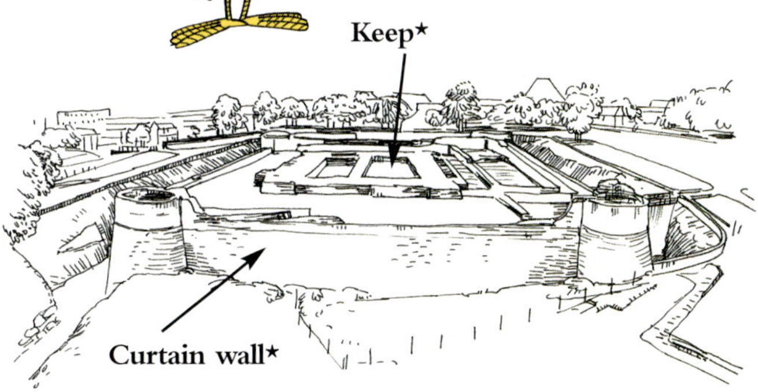

The Ducal Castle

In 1204, the French troops conquered over the dukedom of Normandy. The King of France, Philip Augustus took over the castle and made remarkable transformations. He surrounded the keep* with an enclosure, referred to as a curtain wall*, bordered by a deep moat and including a tower at each angle. He removed the gate next to the keep* and had the Porte des Champs built on the east side of the castle.

5 **Now come down from the ramparts. Leave the ducal palace and find the plaque on your left. Which famous archaeologist carried out excavation work in Caen Castle?**

☐ Arcisse de Caumont ☐ Michel de Boüard ☐ Richard the Lionheart

6 **A little arithmetic: How long did the archaeological excavation work last?**

☐ 24 years

☐ 17 years

☐ 10 years

The archaeological excavations, conducted by Michel de Boüard as from 1956, enabled the vestiges of William the Conqueror's palace and of the keep to be unearthed. The Hall of the Exchequer was also excavated at the same time.

7 **With help from the display panel in front of the Hall of the Exchequer*, find out which king built this edifice.**

Answer: ....

8 **Look carefully at the Hall of the Exchequer* and draw a circle round the four errors in the following drawing.**

He also created two new round towers on the ramparts: the Queen Matilda Tower and the Puchot Tower, linking the castle enclosure to the town ramparts. Between 1417 and 1450, during the Hundred Years' War, the castle was under English domination. To the English, we owe the transformation of the nave of Saint George's church into Gothic style and the construction of Saint Peter's barbican★. In the early 16th Century, considerable earthen embankments were installed alongside the castle walls in the inner enclosure in order to consolidate the castle following the arrival of new gunpowder-based artillery weapons.

9 Now draw the decoration on the Hall of the Exchequer's tympanum (top of the door).

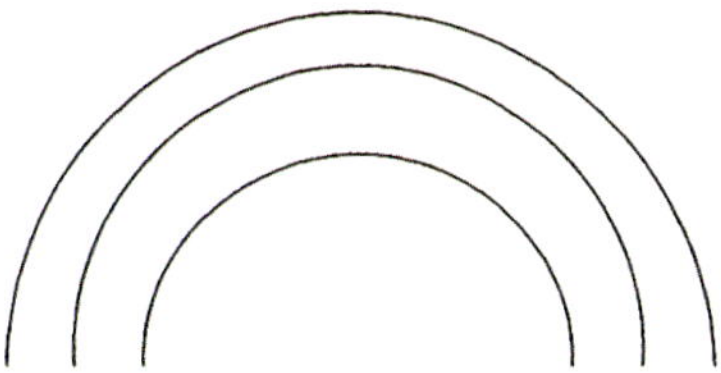

The Hall of the Exchequer welcomed Richard the Lionheart and his barons before they left on their crusade.

10 Now go towards the keep★ curtain wall★. Is there any water in the moat surrounding the wall?

☐ Yes ☐ No

11 Now go on to the Porte des Champs Walk under it and cross the bridge. Take a careful look at the gate. There are five errors in the drawing below. Mark each error with a circle.

12 Does the drawbridge still work?

☐ Yes ☐ No

To reinforce the gate, a fortification referred to as a barbican was built on the outside.

The Ducal Castle

After the Wars of Religion, civilians gradually left the castle where the day-to-day life essentially involved only a modest garrison.
Although the castle escaped destruction during the French Revolution, its keep* was partly destroyed. In the 19th Century, the castle became the *Caserne Lefèbvre* military barracks. The keep*, together with its curtain wall* both completely disappeared.
The castle was only to be given back to civilians after the 1944 bombings.

13 **Among the windows drawn here, draw a circle around the one which resembles those in Saint George's church.**

11th and 12th Centuries **Romanesque style**	15th Century **Flamboyant Gothic style**	16th Century **Renaissance style**

The church still bears the vestiges of the Romanesque architectural style, despite many alterations during the 15th and 16th Centuries. Its bell tower was destroyed in the 18th Century.

14 **Go onto the lawn behind the church and look at the modillions* (sculptures under the roof). Draw the one you prefer in the box below.**

15 **Now go up onto the south rampart and make your way the Queen Matilda Tower. Draw a circle round the loophole* on the following drawing which resembles those on the tower.**

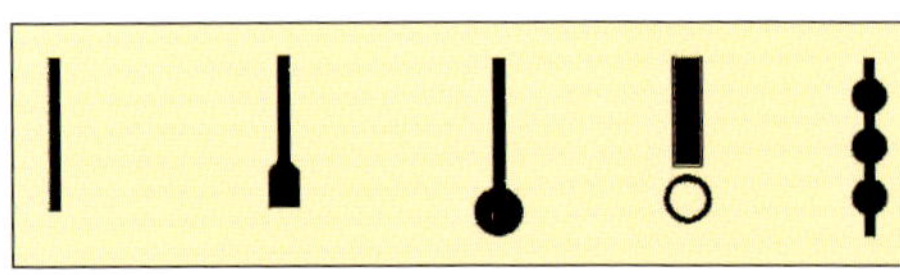

The Queen Matilda Tower (named after William the Conqueror's wife) is one of the castle's round towers built in the 13th Century. The square towers date back to the 12th Century.

Started in 1956, the archaeological excavation work conducted by Michel de Boüard enabled the foundations of the keep★ and its curtain wall★ to be unearthed.

Initially a princely residence, then a fortress and a military barracks, Caen Castle is today a major cultural site. The many monuments that remain from the Middle Ages (the 12th Century Normandy Dukes' Exchequer, Saint George's church, Porte des Champs...) blend in perfect harmony with the Normandy Museum, the Fine Arts Museum and a park adorned with sculptures.

16 What can you see in the port of Caen from the top of the ramparts?

- ☐ Viking long ships
- ☐ Oil tankers
- ☐ Sailing boats
- ☐ Surf boards

From William the Conqueror's reign onwards, boats left this port laden with Caen limestone on their way to England.

Saint Peter's gate existed as early as the 11th Century and provided pedestrian access from the castle to the town of Caen. It was enlarged and fortified with a barbican during the Hundred Years' War.

17 Among the 3 following plans, which one fits with the Saint Peter's gate barbican?

☐ A ☐ B ☐ C

Congratulations!
You have now completed your castle activity trail.

The Men's Abbey

The Men's Abbey is dedicated to Saint Stephen and was founded in 1063 by Duke William. It was inhabited by Benedictine monks* who spent their time praying and studying. It also welcomed pilgrims on their way to the Mont-Saint-Michel. The abbey* is composed of several different elements: the church, referred to as the abbey-church*, is home to William's grave, the cloister and the monastic buildings* where the monks lived and worked.

"Careful, if you want to visit the different abbey rooms, you need to follow the guided tour. Make your way to the Town Council reception, where the guided tours start. You will be given information on opening times and visits. You will also learn that certain rooms may be occupied for weddings or private receptions. Similarly, you will not be allowed to enter the choir* during a religious service. But, don't worry, there are many things to see in the abbey* and the guides will be delighted to show you round. You'll even come face to face with William the Conqueror and you'll learn how the monks lived."*

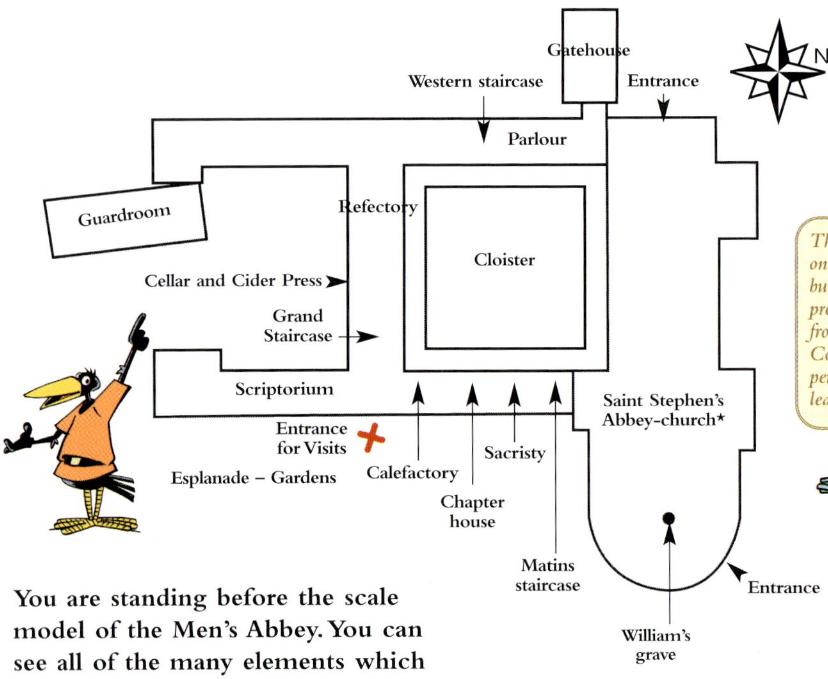

This church is the only remaining building to have preserved elements from William the Conqueror's period. You'll learn more later...

You are standing before the scale model of the Men's Abbey. You can see all of the many elements which form the abbey*. On your map, draw a circle round the abbey-church*.

The present-day buildings were rebuilt during the 18th Century. On the 2nd of November 1790, the monks were driven out by the French Revolution. From 1804 to 1961, the abbey was transformed into a boys' school. Spared during the bombings in June and July 1944, its decorative woodwork and paintings remained intact. Today, the building is home to the Caen town council. Worth a visit: the chapter house, the sacristy, the refectory, the parlour...

Chapter house

1 In this room, where the monks gathered, there is a prior's* stall*. What animal is depicted on the very top?

☐ A horse ☐ A dove ☐ A leopard

As you can see, all of the room's decorative woodwork has been preserved. Did you know that the main function of this woodwork was to isolate the room to protect it from the cold? If you look round, you'll notice that there is no fireplace in this room; the monks didn't heat it.

Former monks' sacristy

2 This is where the monks stored their cloths and liturgical objects.

Who is depicted here?

☐ Jesus and Mary

☐ William and Matilda

☐ A monk and a peasant girl

Matins staircase

3 The matins staircase provided the monks with direct access to the church in the morning.
Look, there's William!
William the Conqueror's head is missing from the mannequin.
Find the head that fits!

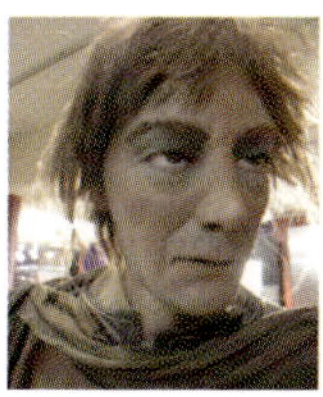

☐ A

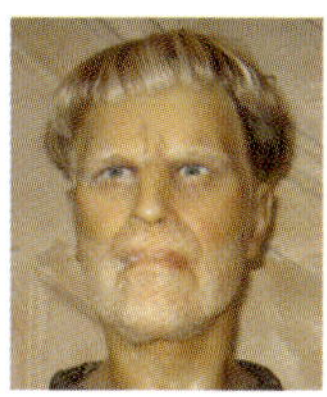

☐ B

☐ C

Just like this mannequin, William was very tall. He measured 10cm more than an average Norman man at the time.

During the day, the monks retired to rest in the cloister, where silence was undoubtedly perfectly respected. From this garden, we can admire the multitude of constructions and reconstructions that have progressively taken place in the Men's Abbey. Nevertheless, the overall aspect is perfectly harmonious and bears witness to the great skill of its builders and stone-cutters.

Cloister

4 You are now in the Men's Abbey cloister.
It was rebuilt during the 18th Century, on the same spot as the former cloister during William's reign. Today, the cloister includes:

- ☐ A fountain
- ☐ Fruit trees
- ☐ A statue of William the Conqueror
- ☐ A garden

In order for the monks to always arrive on time for prayers, work or meals, the time was always marked on the religious service board. It was absolutely necessary, because no one could come and ring a bell in the cloister, since silence was to be respected at all times...

Refectory

5 Now look up and carefully observe the large painting at the far end of the refectory, which is depicted on the right-hand page. This painting by N.B. Lépicié portrays William's landing in England. The copy in this booklet includes 7 deliberate mistakes. Can you find them?

The Benedictine monks were obliged to respect a rule concerning their community life, called the "Rule of Saint Benedict". This rule, for example, ordered them to be obedient and poor, to work, to be punctual, to respect silence... In the refectory, they ate in silence, listening only to the reading of holy texts: hence, they nourished both their soul and their body.

With help from your parents, find the staircase that led to the reader's pulpit*. It's well hidden!

Parlour

6 **This is where the monks welcomed their visitors and could speak to them. What is this room called today?**

- ☐ *Guillaume-le-Conquérant* room
- ☐ *Joseph Poirier* Room
- ☐ *Lanfranc-de-Pavie* room

Because this room is oval, it has a very particular resonance. You will also notice a fireplace.

Clue

The name is written on the wall.

The church facade is a masterpiece of Romanesque architecture and a fine example of a harmonic facade. It is perfectly divided into three levels both vertically and horizontally. The tower spires reach their highest point at 80 metres. As the legend goes, when they collapse, they will bring with them the English monarchy...

Abbey-church - Exterior

7 **Here you are in front of the abbey-church* facade. Take the time to admire this architectural masterpiece that the first Abbot*, Lanfranc had built. Complete the following drawing by adding the missing elements.**

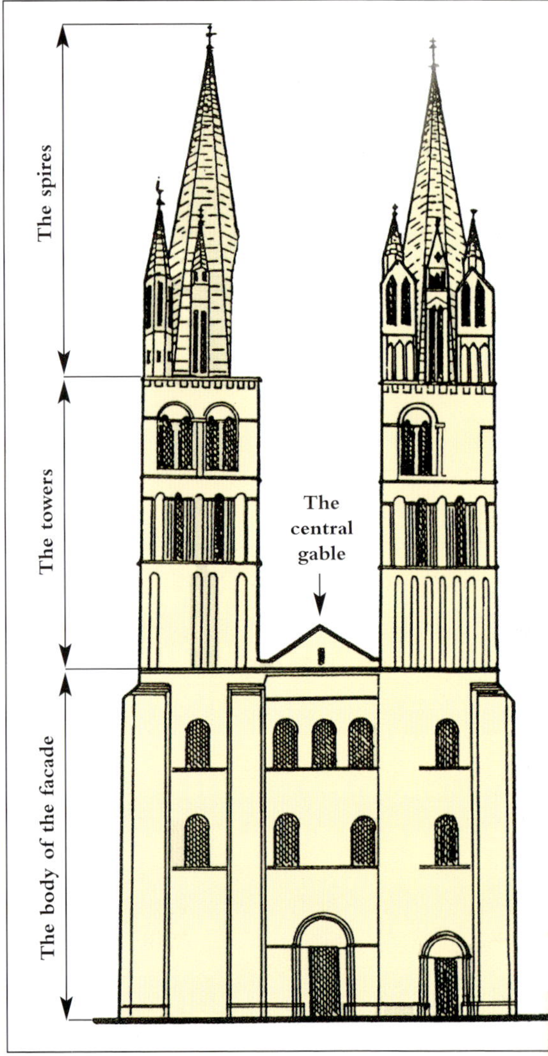

This facade, which was inspired by Jumièges Abbey in the Seine-Maritime region, was in turn a source of inspiration for the architects who designed Notre-Dame de Paris.

Saint Stephen's church is endowed with precious furnishings: organs, paintings, stalls*, stained glass windows... And the choir* is also home to William's grave. The Norman dukes are laid to rest in Rouen or in Fécamp, and the English kings in Westminster. William's desire to be buried in the Men's Abbey bears witness to his affection for his foundation and for the town of Caen.

Now go inside the church, but don't make a noise, because you are in a place of worship! And don't forget that, if there is a religious service, you cannot enter the choir*; you will have to stay at the foot of the nave.

Abbey-church - Interior

8 Inside the church, look carefully at the nave. How many levels does it comprise?

☐ 1 level ☐ 2 levels ☐ 3 levels

☐ 4 levels ☐ 5 levels

This arrangement can be found in many other churches in England, dating from the same period.

It's just for the fun, there are no questions...

If the sacristy is open, you will be able to see a portrait of William. Should it be closed, you can still admire the portrait on one of the postcards for sale. And you will also find it on page 20 of this booklet.

9 Now make your way to the church choir*, where you'll find William the Conqueror's grave. As you can see, it is a very simple marble stone with a Latin inscription.

With the help of Sherlock's clues, can you figure out the date engraved on the gravestone?

Date: ....

What does this date refer to?

Answer: ....

Clues

M = 1000
C = 100
L = 50
X = 10
V = 5
I = 1

Listen carefully to your guide if you want to know the secret of William's grave...

Perched on a rocky outcrop* overlooking the surrounding valleys, Falaise Castle was built a little before the year 1000. It dominated the town which became one of Normandy's major cities. This is where William was born around Christmas 1027. The fortress was already endowed with a stone rampart. Today, there are very few remaining traces of constructions dating back to William's period. The castle, as it stands today, dates essentially from the 12th and 13th Centuries. As a place of power, in the Middle Ages it combined both a military and residential function.

You are now in the castle's reception hall, marked with a cross on your map. This activity booklet's suggested visit is to be made with your accompanying adult(s). It follows the same route as the castle's own audio-guided visit. So you can find your bearings by following both the instructions in your activity booklet and those provided in the guide entitled "guide to the animated visit" which is given to your parents. Thanks to your headphones, you will be told a number of stories in the keeps*. Listen to them carefully; they'll help you to answer the questions in your booklet. Have a nice visit!

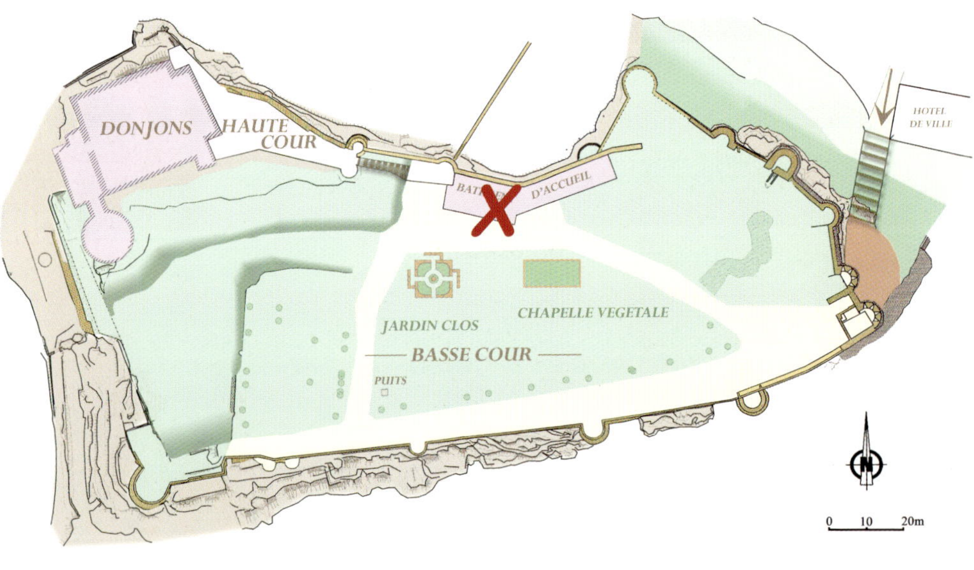

The Great Keep* was built around 1123 by Henry I Beauclerc, William the Conqueror's fourth son, Duke of Normandy and King of England. It was very solid and was used as a refuge in the case of attack, but also as the duke's palace when he visited the town of Falaise. At the same period, Henry built a keep identical to the one in Caen Castle, of which traces are still visible. The keep* entrance was initially protected by a forebuilding. It must have been very solid to resist attack. The present-day grey construction reminds us of the existence of this building.

The Great Keep

Go into the main courtyard and stop for a second. If you turn your back on the reception building, you will see a large construction in the form of a cube: it's the Great Keep*. In order to make your way inside, you need to go through the grey building in front: the forebuilding.

The present-day grey construction reminds us of the existence of the original forebuilding.

1. **What materials were used to build the present-day forebuilding?**

   ☐ Wood and cob

   ☐ Metal and concrete

   ☐ Stone and bricks

2. **Do you think this construction dates from the Middle Ages?**

   ☐ Yes ☐ No

During the Middle Ages, the first floor of the Great Keep* was used as a palace for the duke-king during his frequent visits to Falaise. At the time, the important lords moved permanently around their vast territories in order to govern over them as best they could. So, they had many castles and palaces within which they resided one after another. All of their furniture travelled with them from one residence to the next! These trips enabled them to appear

In the Great Keep: the dukes' palace

Now go up the forebuilding stairs and enter the Great Keep*.

During the Middle Ages, the first floor of the Great Keep was used as a palace for the duke during his frequent visits to Falaise.*

You are now inside the first of the Great Keep's* rooms: the *aula*.

This was a public room and was used for all of the duke-king's official duties (assemblies, judgements, hearings and festivities).

3 Although less modern than present-day houses, these palace's were neverthe-less relatively comfortable. In the following list, tick the facilities that can be found in Falaise Castle's Great Keep*:

☐ Washbasins ☐ Latrines (toilets) ☐ Carpets

Now go through the door at the far left side of the *aula* from the entrance, and go down the stairs which lead to the Small Keep*.

before their subjects and to demonstrate their riches and their power. This keep* was built around the mid 12th Century in order to protect the castle's west side and to enlarge the dukes' residence. You will notice how elegant and comfortable this room appears. The Small Keep* was built during the reign of a duke who was William the Conqueror's grandson. Just like William, he was Duke of Normandy and King of England. His name was Henry II Plantagenet.

The Small Keep

Put your headphones on and listen carefully to the story you are told in this room. Then answer the following questions:

In 1159, which Duke of Normandy and his wife came to Falaise, together with their court, for a festive gathering?

☐ William the Conqueror and Matilda of Flanders
☐ Philip Augustus and Ingeburg of Denmark
☐ Henry Plantagenet and Eleanor of Aquitaine

5 **What were they celebrating?**

☐ Christmas ☐ Easter ☐ The New Year

Now leave the Small Keep*. Make your way along the long corridor to the left of the fireplace towards the Talbot Tower, the castle's third keep*.

This strong tower was built in 1207 by the King of France, who had taken possession of Normandy from the King of England and Duke of Normandy, John Lackland, in 1204. It was not used as a place of residence, but only as a refuge for the castle's soldiers in the case of attack. On the different levels, you will see the wooden floors which enable the overall construction to be lightened, and the stone fire-resistant vaults.

The Talbot Tower

6 **Find the name of the king who built this tower, by figuring out the following riddle:**

My first sounds like the 6th letter of the alphabet
My second is French for « he »
My third is a (not very) important person
My whole is the name of the King of France who took Normandy from the King of England.

Clue

This king was nicknamed Augustus.

You will now return to the Great Keep* via a patio to find yourself inside a room referred to as the camera.

The camera

7 **After reading the display panel, explain what this room was used for at the time of the dukes:**

The room was used: ______________________________

Now make your way to the far right end of the camera and enter the chapel.

The chapel

8 **After reading the display panel, answer the following question: what language was used to read Mass in the Middle Ages?**

Clue

It was also the language used by the Romans.

☐ Ancient Greek
☐ Hebrew
☐ Latin

This was a private chapel, reserved for the duke-king and his close family and companions. It is of Romanesque style, which is easy to recognise because of its round vaults and windows.

When leaving the castle, you will also notice a large statue of William the Conqueror on horseback. It was created in 1851 by the sculptor Louis Rochet. At the time, William was portrayed with a large Vercingetorix-style moustache, although the 11th Century Normans did not grow moustaches. On the statue's base, you can see six other statues depicting the first Dukes of Normandy, William's ancestors.

You can now go to the Great Keep's* lower room by following the signs marked "*suite de la visite*" from the chapel.

There are no questions for this room, but it is entirely devoted to the story of William the Conqueror.
So, take the time to listen to the story via your headphones and to look at the 15 illustrated panels telling the story of the Conqueror's life.

In the Middle Ages, this room was used to store weapons and food supplies. It was also equipped with an oven for cooking bread and a tank to collect rain water.

William the Conqueror's equestrian statue

9 **Write the name of each duke as written in French on the statue. The dates given refer to their reign. Certain letters of their names have been given to help you.**

911-933
R _ _ _ _ _

933-942
G _ _ _ _ _ _ _ _
L _ _ _ _ _
- É _ _ _

942-996
R _ _ _ _ _ _
S _ _ _ P _ _ _

996-1026
R _ _ _ _ _ _
L _ B _ _

1026-1027
R _ _ _ _ _ _
T _ _ _ _

1027-1035
R _ _ _ _ _
L _ M _ _ _ _ F _ _ _ _

GUILLAUME
LE CONQUÉRANT
1035-1087

Congratulations! You have now answered all of the questions on Falaise Castle. Thanks for your visit and see you soon.

Words

ABBEY-CHURCH: a church in an abbey essentially used by nuns and monks for religious services.

ABBOT / ABBESS: the head nun or monk in charge of the abbey. He / she is called father / mother by the other nuns and monks.

ABBEY OR MONASTERY: all of the buildings within which the men and women who have chosen community life and devotion to God (through prayer, mass...) pray and work.
The men are called monks or friars and the women are called cloistered nuns or simply nuns. Within the community, the monks are called brothers and the nuns sisters.

BARBICAN: fortified construction placed in front of a door or gate to defend it.

MONASTIC OR CONVENTUAL BUILDINGS: buildings within which the nuns and monks live and work. They comprise: a refectory, kitchens, a meeting room, a study room, a library, dormitories...

BENEDICTINE: monk / cloistered nun living in community according to a rule referred to as the Rule of Saint Benedict.

PULPIT: a raised tribune from which the monk or nun reads religious texts or gives instructions.

CURTAIN WALL: enclosure (rampart) surrounding the keep.

CHOIR: part of the abbey-church where monks sit for the celebration of religious services.

CONSECRATION: the moment when religious ceremonies can take place and during which the church becomes a sacred place.

KEEP: a castle's main tower. The keep could have many functions: military, residential, surveillance and defence.

ROCKY OUTCROP: rocky headland or point.

HALL: from the Latin *aula*. The palace's reception hall.

LOOPHOLE: opening which was used to throw projectiles, arrows for example, on assailants whilst remaining sheltered.

MODILLION: sculpted stones on the outside of a building roof and sustaining it.

PERJURY: failure to respect a sworn promise or oath.

PRIOR: the community's leading monk. He helps the abbot to manage the abbey.

HALL OF THE EXCHEQUER: large hall in Caen Castle which was used as a reception room, a courtroom and a revenue court.

STALL: a monk's seat which can be seen, in particular, in the abbey-church choir.

TYMPANUM: sculptured decoration above a door.